Row a
By Liza Charlesworth

ISBN: 978-1-339-02784-5

Art Director: Tannaz Fassihi; Designer: Tanya Chernyak
Photos © Getty Images and Shutterstock.com.
Copyright © Liza Charlesworth. All rights reserved. Published by Scholastic Inc.

1 2 3 4 5 6 7 8 9 10   68   32 31 30 29 28 27 26 25 24 23

Printed in Jiaxing, China. First printing, August 2023.

Row, row, row!
It's fun to row a boat.
You can cross a big lake.

It's fun to float in a boat.
You can sit and chat.
You can fish with poles.

This boat has five sails.
Did you know it will go
when the wind blows?

A boat can be fast.
Zip, zap!

A boat can be slow.
It can go with the flow.

A boat can make a lot of foam.

It can go in ice and snow. Brrrrrrrrrrrr!

You can ride in a small boat.
You can spot a whale
that waves its tail!

You can ride in a huge boat.
You can go to a coast with homes.
It is so fun to roam!